And Somewhere, You Knew

Poems from the place in me that's always been yours

Vriti Madaan

For my Nani Maa,

The world doubted me, but you never did. Your love and faith still guide me. This is for you—always. ♥

Dedication

For my parents and friends —
your love, presence, and quiet encouragement
have been the roots beneath these words.
Thank you for being my support.

To *my didi and Rishu—*
for their unwavering love and presence,
a bond that time and distance can never change.

To *my Vee Bee—*
for being there in ways that needed no explanation,
for the laughter, the silences,
and the kind of understanding that asks for nothing.
Your presence shaped more than you know. You may
never know the weight of your presence, but I do. And
that is enough.

And to *my Kysha—*
a piece of my heart in the smallest hands,
my niece, my little joy—
someone I'll always hold close, no matter where life takes us.

Contents

Acknowledgment

This book would not have been possible without the love and support of those who stood by me through every written word, every doubt, and every quiet moment of creation.

To my parents—thank you for being my foundation, for believing in me even when I questioned myself, and for giving me the space to grow into my voice.

To *my didi and Rishu*—your encouragement, your strength, and the warmth of our bond have been a constant source of reassurance. The ones who have always stood by me with unwavering love and strength. Your wisdom, kindness, and belief in me have been my anchor through every storm and my cheer through every victory. Thank you for being my safe place, my guide, and my forever home in a world that constantly shifts. I am endlessly grateful for you.

To *my Vee Bee*, My Constant Listener—your quiet understanding, your presence, and the way you always showed up without being asked gave me the courage to write this book. Some of these words exist because of you. Someone who will always be a part of the stories I tell, whether they know it or not. For the moments, and the conversations —thank you for being there in ways that mattered. Some people leave footprints; some just leave warmth. You did both.

To Kysha—my little ray of sunshine, whose tiny hands hold a piece of my heart. Your innocence and laughter remind me why stories matter.

And to every reader who finds a reflection of themselves in these pages—this book belongs to you just as much as it belongs to me.

With gratitude,
Vriti Madaan

Preface

There is a certain kind of love that does not ask for attention.

It stays quiet. Listens. Lingers.

This collection began quietly —

in half-written thoughts, notes on my phone,

and the spaces between conversations.

These poems are for the moments that didn't ask to be understood — just felt.

If this book finds you at a time when you need comfort,

clarity, or simply a reminder that it's okay to feel deeply —

I hope it sits gently with you.

Thank you for being here.

But some stories need more than poetry. And now, **Mira** will finally tell you hers

— VRITI

Before You Begin

Words have always been easier for me on paper than in conversation. I have written about love, about loss, about the quiet ache of waiting for something unspoken. And yet, I have never told this story—at least, not in full.

This book is not just poetry. It is a dedication. A collection of all the things I never had the courage to say. To him. To myself. To anyone who has ever stayed, even when they weren't sure if they should.

Maybe one day, I'll tell the whole story. Maybe one day, he'll finally understand.

But for now, this is what remains.

— Mira

Chapter 1

Sometimes, words arrive as whispers—soft, fleeting. Others demand to be written, spoken and heard. I have always believed that words find us before we are ready for them. This book is filled with words I never dared to say out loud, words that felt heavier when they remained unspoken.

My fingers trace the keyboard, typing the title: And Somewhere, You Knew. The bold letters stare back at me, a silent testament to everything left unsaid. My second poetry collection after The Way You Felt Like Home. This one is different. Heavier. More personal. It is not just a book—it is a dedication. A confession in disguise. A letter that may never be read by the one it was written for.

My name sits at the bottom of the Author's Note. Mira. The girl who stayed.

The publishing house hums with quiet efficiency. Stacks of manuscripts clutter desks, editors pace between meetings, and the rhythmic tapping of keyboards fills the air. A world full of stories—some unfinished, some waiting to be told, some waiting to be read. And yet, the one story I have carried the longest remains untold, buried somewhere between the notes on my phone.

A soft chime pulls me back. A message. My heart stumbles before my mind can remind it not to. But it isn't him.

Of course not.

I exhale, leaning back in my chair. I don't know why I still expect him to reach out first. He never does.

And yet, he is always there, too. He never truly leaves. And I don't want him to. He has been there through it all. I have made peace with our patterns.

My fingers hover over the keyboard as I type the dedication page, my emotions still raw:

For the ones who stayed. And for the ones who knew they did.

Maybe one day, he will read between the lines.

Maybe one day, he will understand.

But for now, this is enough.

Chapter 2

My second home—the publishing house—is more than just a workplace; it is a maze of stories waiting to be unraveled, a home for words that demand to be heard. Somewhere between the scent of freshly printed manuscripts and the hum of the coffee machine, I have built a life that feels steady, even when my heart is not. This place has given me the courage to publish what I once thought belonged only to my phone.

I arrange the drafts of my manuscript on the desk, running my fingers over the printed pages. The final edits are due soon. Each poem feels like a piece of me, laid bare, waiting to be judged, understood, or perhaps even misunderstood. And somewhere in those interpretations, I wonder if someone—if *he*—will recognize himself.

"Lost in thought again?"

My colleague, Naina, leans against my desk, sipping her coffee. "I swear, Mira, you have a habit of disappearing into your own head."

I smile, tucking a strand of hair behind my ear. "Occupational hazard."

She glances at the manuscript. "This one's different, isn't it?"

I hesitate before nodding. "Yeah."

There's a weight to this book that wasn't there before. My last collection was about nostalgia and belonging. This one is about the things I could never say aloud. About a boy who was always just out of reach. About love that was never spoken but always felt.

A buzz from my phone draws my attention. A name I haven't seen in months flashes across the screen.

Aiden.

My breath catches. I don't open the message immediately. Instead, I let the moment linger, let the emotions rise and settle before I gather the courage to see what he has to say.

And just like that, the distance between us feels smaller and heavier, all at once.

I stare at the message, my fingers hovering over the screen. A simple *Hey* stares back at me. Just three letters, but they hold too much weight. I exhale, setting my phone face-down on the desk.

"What's wrong?" Naina asks, watching me closely.

"Nothing," I reply, forcing a smile. But she doesn't buy it.

"It's him, isn't it?"

I don't answer, but my silence is enough.

"You know you don't have to keep doing this to yourself," she says, softer this time.

"I know," I whisper. But knowing and feeling are two different things.

Chapter 3

I never intended for this book to be about him.

That's what I told myself at first. That this would be a collection about healing, about solitude, about the little moments I found my strength again. But the more I wrote, the more the truth bled through—I wasn't writing about healing, I was writing about longing. About him.

The kind that doesn't announce itself. The kind that grows in the silences between conversations and settles in the spaces no one sees.

I didn't even realize how much of him lived in these pages until I started reading them aloud to myself.

The way I described hands—his.

The way I talked about distance—ours.

The way I kept returning to the idea of waiting.

The thing is... we never even had a beginning. Not a proper one. And maybe that's what haunted me most. There was no defining moment I could point to, no dramatic confession, no heartbreak to make sense of. Just a string of almosts, and a quiet thread that pulled me back to him again and again.

We were always too polite. Too careful. Best friends, from a distance. Close enough to feel real. Distant enough to never be certain.

I remember the first time we reconnected after years apart. The way he smiled like nothing had changed. How easily he slipped into conversation, like we hadn't spent years talking only in fragments. There was always something unsaid hanging between us. A strange familiarity, like a book I had read once and misplaced, only to find it again—creased at the parts that mattered most.

I would never call it love. Not in the traditional sense. But it was something. Something real enough to keep me up some nights, wondering if he ever thought about me the way I thought about him. If he ever replayed those eye contact moments that felt like they carried entire chapters between them.

The message that day—it had arrived when I least expected it. The same time I was struggling with the final section of this manuscript. A strange coincidence, or maybe the universe just has a twisted sense of timing.

His name flashed across my phone.

Aiden.

I didn't open it right away. I rarely did. There was always a hesitation with him—a need to preserve the feeling longer than the conversation. Because sometimes, the hope felt better than the reality.

Naina noticed. She always did.

"It's him, isn't it?"

I didn't answer, but my silence was enough.

"You know you don't have to keep doing this to yourself," she said, her voice softer than usual.

"I know," I whispered.

But knowing and feeling are two different things. And some feelings never go away. They just change shape. Sometimes they turn into poems.

This book became the space I couldn't find with him. A space where I could finally be honest—not with him, but with myself. The poems here aren't just metaphors. They're my truths dressed in rhythm. They're the questions I never asked, the versions of us I imagined, the pauses between his replies.

I wrote this book because I didn't know how else to let go.

Or maybe I didn't want to.

Maybe part of me still thinks he'll pick it up someday, read between the lines, and finally see everything I was too afraid to say.

And if he doesn't?

Then I hope someone else does. I hope someone who once stayed too long, or waited too quietly, or loved too silently finds their reflection in these verses.

Because at the end of it all, maybe this book isn't just about him.

Maybe it's about anyone who's ever loved in silence and dared to write it down.

Chapter 4

There's something sacred about poetry.

It doesn't ask for permission. It doesn't wait for clarity.
It arrives, like a storm or a whisper, and demands to be felt.

When I began writing these poems, I didn't intend for them to become a book. They were my way of making sense of the ache I couldn't name. Of understanding why some silences were heavier than goodbyes. Why certain people take up space in your life even when they're rarely present in it.

These poems came to life in the quietest corners of my days—in the backseat of a taxi, in the lonely glow of 2 a.m., in the space between his message and my reply. I wrote them when I didn't know how to talk about him. When I wasn't even sure I was allowed to.

And still, he was in every line.

Aiden never asked to be the muse. He probably doesn't even know he is.

But I think some people are written into your story long before either of you realize it. Not because of grand gestures or romantic declarations—but because of the little moments they unknowingly hold you through.

There were days when I resented how much space he occupied in my heart. And days when I was grateful for it—because even in his absence, he gave me something to write about.

But this book isn't just about him.

It's about me. About staying. About choosing presence in a world of vanishing acts. About holding space for feelings I didn't know what to do with.

It's about friendship that slips into something deeper, about glances that last too long, about what we carry when nothing is said but everything is felt.

If you've ever stayed for someone who didn't know you were waiting...

If you've ever loved without needing to be loved back the same way...

If you've ever been the quiet one who notices everything...

This book is for you.

Each poem is a fragment—of memory, of longing, of unspoken truths.

They aren't chronological. Some of them might contradict each other. But that's the nature of love, isn't it? Messy, layered, uncertain.

Maybe, somewhere in these pages, you'll find pieces of yourself.

Maybe you'll find someone you once knew.

Or maybe... you'll finally understand why you stayed.

So go ahead.

Read slowly.
Read tenderly.
Read as if you've written these words in another lifetime.

Let them become yours.

Love them like your own.

The Way the Silence Spoke

It was in the quiet words you never read,
it wasn't in the things you said.
A pause, a look, a softer blink,
you said more than you'd ever think.

The silence wasn't empty space,
it held a calm, a kind of grace.
Just you and I, the evening slow,
with all the things we'll never show.

That night, no plans, no words to spend,
just coffee, music, and a friend.
Your gaze met mine, the moment stayed—
time forgot to slip away.

The crowd around, the noise, the light,
yet somehow we just felt so right.
You didn't speak, but still I heard,
a language deeper than a word.

We were closer than we knew

You sat just two roll calls from me,
but still felt like a mystery.
Three years we shared the same old space,
yet never truly left a trace.

You were the boy who ruled the scene,
all mischief loud and far from clean.
I kept my distance, head held high,
no reason then to wonder why.

You chased the world, I read my part,
no story then to even start.
Just faces in a hallway blur,
no tug, no thought, no whispered stir.

I never thought you'd be the one
to light my sky when day was done.
But slowly, through the years we grew,
and we were closer than we knew.

Now when I think of all that time,
those silent years, that missed-out rhyme,
I smile and let the moment stay—
Some stories bloom the quiet way.

   And Somewhere, You Knew

It Started so small

We walked away from school and time,
each chasing dreams in separate rhymes.
New cities came, new stories grew,
and life moved on — as it should do.

No letters sent, no words exchanged,
our chapters turned, our worlds rearranged.
No bond, no thread, no tale to spin,
just echoes where we both had been.

Then one day, lost in chatter's scroll,
your message sparked without a goal—
No reason clear, no meaning deep,
just something time had left to keep.

I typed a yes, and that was all,
no spark, no rise, no sudden call.
Just something small, a simple start,
that somehow moved the gears of heart.

We spoke, we laughed, then moved along,
no strings, no silence stretched too long.
But now I see that even then,
the quiet wrote us in the end.

I never knew that one small thread
would stitch you back in all I said.
But life is quiet when it's kind—
it brings back those you're meant to find.

Back Then, It Was Nothing

Back then, it wasn't warm or deep,
just borrowed words we'd barely keep.
You'd text when something came your way,
a task, a note, a form to say.

I answered quick, then disappeared,
no closeness yet, no moment cleared.
We lived in worlds so far apart,
no reason then to share the heart.

I wasn't yours, you weren't mine,
just faces crossing once in time.
Both tied to lives we'd once begun,
not knowing what we'd yet become.

There were no sparks, no playful tone,
just simple chats when you felt alone.
No longing texts, no heart to send—
just moments that would blink and end.

But quiet has its way, I've learned,
it waits, it watches, then returns.
And somewhere deep in that gray blend,
our silence softened into friend.

Because, I stayed

The storms had passed, the chapters closed,
on hearts once open, now reposed.
We'd both let go, we'd both moved through,
what lingered still was something new.

We weren't the kind to chase or call,
but silence never meant to fall.
A meme, a thought, some passing news,
small strings we didn't think we'd choose.

I reached a little more each day,
with stories, gossip, jokes to say.
And slowly then, without a cue,
you said, "This friendship stayed... 'cause of you."

Not fate, not chance, not something planned,
just footsteps drawn back to the sand.
The kind of bond that doesn't fade,
the kind that lingers—because I stayed.

  And Somewhere, You Knew

The Gossip Got Us Talking

We weren't the kind who talked a lot,
just now and then, when something caught.
No stories shared, no hearts on sleeve,
just passing days with no real weave.

Until one day, a message flew—
"Guess what I heard?"—I typed back too.
One whisper led to two, then more,
and suddenly, silence was out the door.

You laughed at things I had to say,
old school tea, the news today.
And just like that, without a plan,
we found a rhythm — oh, how it ran.

We weren't yet close, but inch by inch,
you'd linger more, you wouldn't flinch.
But something sparked, light and true,
in every "Did you hear that too?"

Vriti Madaan   33

You never said Much

You never said much, barely a line,
but there I was, talking like it's a sign.
You'd nod or laugh, just enough to stay,
while I kept yapping the day away.

I told you stories, some wild, some true,
from midnight dreams to déjà vu
You listened more than you replied,
a quiet space where I could hide.

Your silence wasn't cold or far—
it felt like sitting beneath a star.
Not loud, not bright, but somehow always there,
a constant kind of subtle care.

I never minded that you spoke less,
somehow, your quiet said it best.
While I would dance with words and whim,
you'd smile and let the light grow dim.

And Then You Spoke

For months I spoke, and you just heard—
no deep confessions, not one bold word.
You'd nod, you'd smile, you'd let me be,
a quiet wall that steadied me.

But then one day, a message stayed—
not something planned, not something swayed.
A thought you had, a dream once chased,
a piece of you, no longer cased.

It wasn't loud, no fire, no show,
but in your way, it let me know.
A shift so small, yet something stirred—
you finally gave me your first word.

I read it once, and then once again,
like gentle drops of summer rain.
No need to speak a thousand things—
your silence now had quiet wings.

You spoke, and I just sat in awe,
each word you gave, unwrapped and raw.
You didn't say the world to me—
but carved a space where you could be.

⋯⊷⊶⋯

Vriti Madaan   35

You didn't drift

You weren't the type to text each day,
no morning words or long cliché.
But somehow, you were always there—
like breath—unseen, but in the air.

A message when the skies turned grey,
a call that somehow knew the day.
No fleeting words, no show, no sign,
just steady presence—soft, yet mine.

You didn't drift the way most do—
not always near, but never through.
And in a world that fades and goes,
you felt like home the silence knows.

Not always close, not always near,
but never once did you disappear.
And that alone, I came to see,
was all the proof you cared for me.

 And Somewhere, You Knew

The Gossip Kept Us Going

It wasn't talks of dreams or pain,
just silly things that felt insane.
A meme, a reel, some harmless tea—
you laughed, and then replied to me.

No midnight calls, no whispered fears,
just rumors spun through passing years.
A text, a joke, a name we knew—
small echoes pulling me to you.

No deep confessions, no clear plan,
just "Did you hear about that man?"
You'd roll your eyes, I'd send a gif,
and just like that, we'd start our shift.

Some friendships bloom in silent nights,
some glow in gossip, jokes, and bites.
We weren't the kind who always knew—
but laughter made the bond feel true.

So there we were, just back again,
not lovers, no, just perfect friends.
And looking back, I think I see—
you stayed because I spilled the tea.

Everything Our Eyes Held

In a crowded café, lost in the sound,
our eyes had found their own way around.
A second held, a moment passed—
somehow, our eyes would always ask.

You always knew when something pained,
when I withdrew, when I remained.
You never said it, never asked,
but in your gaze, I felt unmasked.

I never sat with them, just you,
behind your seat, the same old view.
And when our eyes met in the glass,
I turned away—but why so fast?

Maybe you knew, or maybe not,
but even now, I hold that thought.
Of all the words we left unsaid,
our eyes still speak inside my head.

You must have known—it's in my eyes,
the quiet truths, the soft goodbyes.
The things I never dared to say,
but somehow hoped you knew anyway.

The Things You Never Noticed

You spoke of her, or maybe them,
so easily, like drifting stems.
I smiled, I laughed—played my part,
but something ached beneath my heart.

Did you notice? Did you see—
how my laughter turned carefully?
How I smiled too wide in selfies clicked,
as if the light could hide the twist?

You never asked for pictures we took,
not once, not twice, not a second look.
And though I knew, I wished you'd see,
that little sting it left in me.

And still, our eyes would find their stay,
a fleeting glance that meant to stray.
You never asked, you never knew,
but somewhere, somehow, I hope you do.

Vriti Madaan   39

The Quiet Truth

I never asked, I never said,
just smiled too wide and turned my head.
You talked of plans, of someone new,
and I just hoped you never knew.

Maybe it's me, or maybe not,
but if you're happy, that's my lot.
And if she holds what I once dreamed,
I'll learn to love you from between.

You never saw the words I hid,
the way my eyes would close a bit.
The times I stayed, the times I knew,
the way my world revolved near you.

And if one day we grow apart,
just know—you were my favorite part.
Not in a way the world could see,
but in the way you looked at me.

Still Smiling

It starts with a buzz, a quiet glow,
your name appearing—like you'd know.
No reason why, no grand affair,
yet somehow, I pause and stare.

And then, a photo flickers through,
a memory framed in shades of you.
A passing scroll, a glance so bright,
but tell me why it feels so right?

Some days, it's random—just your face,
or moments time refused to chase.
And there I am, caught off my guard,
grinning wide, my heart disarmed.

I never tell you—why would I?
It's just a thought that rushes by.
Yet here I sit, a little fool,
smiling like you set the rule.

The Eyes That Stayed

You stood there, suitcase by your side,
a moment stretched, yet undefined.
No words were said, no sighs, no tears,
just silence heavy with the years.

My eyes stayed dry, they wouldn't fall,
but still, they spoke—perhaps too small.
Did you see the weight they bore?
Did you feel what I ignored?

Somewhere between a wave and stare,
I wonder—was it just the air?
Or did you pause, just for a beat,
like something pulled beneath your feet?

You left, and still, I stand the same,
not sure if you had known my name—
not just the sound, but all I meant,
the words my quiet gaze had sent.

The Hug We Never Shared

Maybe we should have hugged that day,
before the miles pulled you away.
Maybe your arms could've made me stay—
not in place, but in some quiet way.

A second more, a breath held tight,
a moment that could've felt so right.
Maybe then, when the distance grew,
I wouldn't have felt I was losing you.

And even now, after all these years,
Why do we hold back, weighed by fears?
Is it something we both just know—
a truth unspoken, left to grow?

Not in words, not in name,
but something shifted, not the same.
And maybe a hug—just one, just then—
could have kept me whole again.

A Memory, Still Parked

We sat in silence, just us two,
beneath the sky so vast and blue.
The world kept moving, yet we stayed,
lost in the words we'd never trade.

No rush to go, no need to run,
just sitting there, the night begun.
His voice was calm, his eyes sincere,
a place I'd always hold so dear.

He listened close, he always knew,
the weight behind the words I threw.
And in his gaze, I swear I saw,
a space where I could rest my awe.

The car stood still, the city glowed,
but time itself had barely flowed.
A moment small, yet vast and free—
a memory that stays with me.

When My Prayers Reach You

I pray for you more than I pray for me,
in whispered words the world won't see.
For joy to find you where you stand,
for fate to hold your heart in hand.

I ask the stars to light your way,
to ease your nights, to bless your day.
To calm the storms before they start,
to wrap you safe, to guard your heart.

I pray the mornings feel like home,
that laughter finds you when you roam.
That strength holds firm when days are long,
that kindness meets you, soft yet strong.

I ask the moon to watch you sleep,
to hush the thoughts that cut too deep.
To keep you safe when roads turn dim,
to guard your light when hope runs thin.

You'll never hear the words I send,
but may they reach like a quiet wind.
And when the weight feels hard to bear,
I hope you feel my presence there.

No need to ask, no need to see,
but if you're warm, then so am I.
For love like this makes no demands—
it only stays, it understands.

The One Exception

I sigh, I rant, I roll my eyes,
laying bare the world's disguise.
The way they act, the words they feign,
the hollow games that feel the same.

He listens close, he lets me speak,
no rush to fix, no urge to preach.
A quiet nod, a knowing glance,
as if he reads between the stance.

"They're all the same," I claim once more,
he only smiles, says nothing more.
But in his silence, something stays—
a warmth that cuts through all my haze.

For every name I brush aside,
for every flaw I can't abide,
he stays, untouched, he doesn't wane—
the only one who feels the same.

And maybe he will never see,
the only one I like is he.

And Somewhere, You Knew

I never said it, not in words,
but silence spoke, and you had heard.
The way my gaze would hold, then stray,
the things my laughter hid away.

I never asked, yet you just knew,
when space was best, when to pull through.
No words were sworn, no vows in view
just knowing smiles that paved the way they knew.

I never clung, I never claimed,
yet every thought still breathed your name.
Through fleeting looks and quiet sighs,
I wonder—did you read my eyes?

And if one day our paths divide,
if time and fate pull us aside,
I hope you'll pause and somehow see,
you always meant the most to me.

And maybe I won't ever say,
but somewhere, somehow, you knew anyway.

I Hope You Watch Me

I hope you watch me when I speak,
when words spill out, fast and free.
When I forget to filter thought from sound,
and let my laughter twirl around.

I hope you see the way I glow,
caught in stories you may not know.
The way my hands paint through the air,
as if the world is waiting there.

I wonder if you ever stare,
not just at words, but all laid bare.
At how my heart peeks through my speech,
in ways my silence couldn't reach.

I'll never ask, I'll never say,
but maybe you watch me anyway.
And somewhere, somehow, you just knew—
every word was meant for you.

Vriti Madaan

Bonus: The Things I Loved Most

There was always something about him—something quiet, something certain. Maybe it was the way his eyes held entire conversations without ever speaking, or the way his smile could turn an ordinary moment into something I'd remember forever.

His eyes, deep and knowing, carried things he'd never say out loud. They saw me in ways I didn't even see myself. And his smile—rare, but when it came, it felt like sunlight breaking through the coldest days.

I don't know if he ever noticed how much these small things meant to me. But somewhere, I hope he knew.

1. The Way His Eyes Spoke

I've seen the world in shades of blue,
but never quite the way he knew.
A fleeting glance, a gaze held tight,
his eyes could turn the dark to light.

They spoke of things he'd never say,
of restless dreams and skies so gray.
But somewhere deep, beyond their hue,
they whispered softly, I see you.

No need for words, no grand display,
just quiet looks that made me stay.
And even now, through time and space,
I swear I still can see his face.

⸺◦⸺

2. The Smile I Never Forgot

His smile was never loud or bright,
just soft—a warmth, a touch of light.
Not meant for all, not always there,
but when it was, I wished to stare.

It wasn't built to steal the show,
but somehow, still, it made me glow.
A grin, a smirk, just something small,
yet somehow, it would say it all.

I wonder now, does he still know,
the way his smile could steal the show?
Or was it just for me to see,
a secret gift the world won't see?

Chapter 5

The poems are out now.

On paper. In print. Breathing on their own.

It's strange—how something so deeply personal can suddenly feel like it belongs to everyone. Readers hold these words in their hands, not knowing how much of my heart they carry.

And still… it feels right.

I no longer flinch when I hear his name. I no longer scroll through old messages trying to read between lines that were never written. Instead, I sit with the silence that follows—and it doesn't ache like it used to.

There's a quiet strength in saying what needed to be said, even if the person you wrote it for never hears it.

Aiden hasn't read the book.

Or maybe he has.

Maybe he's still reading it the way he always reads me—slowly, uncertainly, from a distance.

But I've stopped waiting for him to say something.

Because somewhere along the way, I found my voice.

And now, for the first time, I know what to do with it.

I open a blank document and stare at the blinking cursor.

Not a poem this time. A story.

Ours.

The one I never told fully, not even to myself.

But I will.

When I'm ready.

And I think... I am.

Chapter 6

It wasn't a grand moment.

No confessions. No dramatic gestures.

Just a borrowed umbrella, a train ride, and the way he looked at me like I'd always been there—even when he hadn't.

We were walking back from Ryan's house. Rain tapping gently against the pavement, the kind that doesn't drench you but lingers long enough to feel like memory. Aiden held the umbrella over both of us, but the tilt was subtle—closer to me. He probably didn't even realize.

We talked about nothing important. The weather. A book he half-read. A joke Ryan had cracked. But I remember every word.

Because that was the moment I realized:

I was always waiting for him to look at me like that again.

I haven't written that memory into any poem.

It didn't fit in rhyme or rhythm.

It just... stayed.

Like he always did.

Maybe he always knew.

And maybe he was just afraid.

Or maybe we're still too shy to admit it—even after all these years of friendship.

But if he's reading this now, if these words somehow found their way to him...

Aiden,

Was it ever more than just timing?

Or were we both too careful with something that could've changed everything?

And if you found even one poem that felt like your own... then this book was always meant for you.

A Note from the Author

If you've reached here, thank you—for staying.

This book was never meant to be loud.

It was always meant to be a whisper. A trace of something unspoken. A space between what was and what could have been.

Every poem in these pages carries pieces of silence—words I never said, looks I never explained, and love I never confessed out loud. Not because I didn't feel it, but because I never knew how.

Some stories begin with a hello.

Ours began with quiet.

Maybe that's why it took me so long to tell it.

But I will. One day soon.

I've started writing it, actually. Not as poetry this time, but as the story behind the poems—the chapters we lived without knowing they were becoming a book of their own.

So if you're wondering who Aiden really is, if you're curious about what happened after the poems, or before them...

You'll hear it from me. All of it.

But for now, thank you—for listening to what I couldn't say until now.

With all my heart,

— Mira

When I began writing this collection, I didn't expect Mira to take the lead.

But somewhere between the unwritten confessions and silent connections, she found her way to the page—and stayed.

And Somewhere, You Knew is Mira's voice. Her present. Her way of saying what she never could. A love letter wrapped in metaphors, written for someone who may never realize it was meant for him.

But this is only the beginning of her story.

Soon, you'll meet Mira again.

Not just as the girl who wrote these poems, but as the one who lived through every line.

The novel *The Way She Stayed* will tell you what Mira couldn't say here—how it all began, what she never admitted, and why she stayed through it all.

Until then, I hope these poems found a home in you.

And maybe... reminded you of the words you haven't said yet.

—Vriti